Felton, Harold
Mumbet

DATE DUE

JL 6 '91			
JL 14 '90			

OTHER BOOKS BY HAROLD W. FELTON

MUMBET
THE
STORY OF
ELIZABETH
FREEMAN

Harold W. Felton

ILLUSTRATED BY DONN ALBRIGHT

DODD, MEAD & COMPANY, NEW YORK

To Florence and Ray

CONTENTS

INTRODUCTION

THE MAIN OUTLINE of the story of Elizabeth Freeman, known as Betty, Bet, Bett, Mum Bett, and Mumbet, is well known in the Berkhire Hills of western Massachusetts and northwestern Connecticut. On her gravestone her name is spelled "Mumbet." That is the spelling Catherine Sedgwick used and the one I have adopted. I use "Bet" also to conform to this spelling.

Court records in Great Barrington, Massachusetts, Vol. 4, No. 1, contain a transcript of the proceedings when she, a slave, together with another named Brom, brought an action in 1781 to obtain their freedom under the new constitution of Massachusetts which provided that "all men are created equal." The trial was the third Tuesday in August, 1781.

Bet's lawyer was Theodore Sedgwick, a young man who became a member of the Continental Congress, a congressman, a United States senator, and a judge of the Supreme Court of Massachusetts. He was assisted by Tapping Reeve, a lawyer from Litchfield, Connecticut. It was he who started the first law school in North America in 1784 in a building which still may be seen in Litchfield.

Bet lived in a community that had a long respect for freedom. In the winter of 1772-73 political leaders in Sheffield, Massachusetts, drew up, in the Ashley House where Bet was a slave, the Sheffield Declaration of Independence, which was adopted at a Town Meeting on January 12, 1773. This document has been called America's first "Declaration of Independence."

There was also an antislavery resolution on February 25, 1774. But slavery continued until Bet's determination set a new force for freedom in motion.

The former slave emerged from her historical litigation a free woman, recovering "against the said John Ashley the sum of thirty shillings lawful Silver Money Damages, and the Costs of this Suit Taxed at five pounds fourteen shillings and four pence like Money." John Ashley filed a notice of appeal which he did not pursue.

Apart from her place in history because of her successful law suit and a courageous incident during Shays' Rebellion, Bet won a still greater place in the hearts of the people around her in Great Barrington and Stockbridge.

Her will reveals a daughter named Elizabeth, known as Little

Bet. Her will also discloses that a granddaughter was Marianne Dean. Two great-grandchildren were Mary Elizabeth Dean and Wealthy Ann Dean. Another great-granddaughter was Lydia Maria Ann Van Schaack, and Amos Josiah Van Schaack was a great-grandson.

Henry Dwight Sedgwick, one of Judge Theodore Sedgwick's sons, and a lawyer of considerable reputation, delivered a lecture on "The Practicability of the Abolition of Slavery" at the Lyceum in Stockbridge in February, 1831. He gave a brief outline of Mumbet's biography and said: "She was married when young; her husband died soon after, in the continental service in the revolutionary war, leaving her with one child. During the residue of her life she remained a widow." I have searched the records of Massachusetts men who were in the Continental army but have been unable to identify which one of the many who died, and whose name was Freeman, may have been her husband.

Henry Dwight Sedgwick continued: ". . . without ever claiming superiority, she uniformly, I believe in every case, obtained an ascendancy over all those with whom she was associated in service. Her spirit of fidelity to her employers was such as has never been surpassed. . . . She claimed no distinction, but it was yielded to her from her superior experience, energy, skill and sagacity."

There is abundant testimony of her courage, her good sense, her rare ability in almost every form of daily social and human conduct. By virtue of her care of the Sedgwick children and her occupation of nursing, she became known as Mumbet, a name which reveals the affection she earned.

Mr. Sedgwick made comment of her skill as a nurse: ". . . she had no competitor. I believe she never lost a child, when she had the care of its mother, at its birth. When a child, wailing in the arms of its mother, heard her steps on the stairway, or approaching the door, it ceased to cry."

Catharine, one of the younger Sedgwick children, who became a popular novelist, wrote: "One should have known this remarkable woman, the native majesty of her deportment. . . . Mumbet was the only person who could tranquillize my mother when her mind was disordered—the only one of her friends whom she liked to have about her—and why? She treated her with the same respect she did when she was sane. As far as possible, she obeyed her commands and humored her caprices; in short, her superior instincts hit upon the mode of treatment that science has since adopted."

Henry Dwight Sedgwick gave Mumbet credit for saving his life: "But for the care of one of this calumniated race, I should not now, probably, be living to give this testimony."

Others had similar feelings. Electra Jones, in her book, *Stockbridge, Past and Present*, published in 1854, wrote: "Her usual employment was nursing, in which she was peculiarly skilled."

Mumbet was at the center of all family joy and sorrow in the Sedgwick family, and of much of that of the community. Catharine, in her autobiography, wrote that Mumbet presided at the huge kitchen fire, "Queen of the domain," and she recalled "my love of Mumbet, that noble woman, the main pillar of our household." Catharine put into focus the fine qualities that produced admiration on every hand: "Mumbet had a clear and nice perception of justice, and a stern love of it, an uncompromising honesty in word and deed, and conduct of high intelligence, that made her the unconscious moral teacher of the children she tenderly nursed. . . . I do not believe that any temptation could have induced Mumbet to swerve from the truth. . . . Truth was her nature—the offspring of courage and loyalty."

And Mumbet's reputation did not remain entirely local. Harriet Martineau, the English novelist and political economist, in her book, *Recollections of Western Travels*, commented about her: "A woman once lived in Massachusetts whose name ought to be preserved in all histories of the State as one of its honors, though she was a slave. . . . She was considered as connected with Judge Sedgwick's family after she had left their house for a home of her own. By her great industry and frugality she supported a large family of grandchildren and great-grandchildren. . . . As far as energy and talent are concerned, I should not hesitate to say that in her own sphere Mum Bett had no superior or equal; and the same may be said about the quality of her fidelity."

Mark Hopkins, the educator, was one of her friends and his letters contain frequent references to her as "a Negro woman and former slave and a remarkable character."

The wife of Theodore Sedgwick, Jr., the Judge's oldest son, painted Mumbet's picture. Her daughter, Marie, gave it to the

Massachusetts Historical Society in February, 1884.

Mumbet died in 1829. The Sedgwick family thought she was eighty-five years old. John Ashley, who owned Bet as a slave, married Hannah Hogeboom of Claverack, New York, in 1735. Tradition tells us that Bet was purchased from the Hogebooms and was brought to Ashley Falls at the age of six months. When the known facts and the legends and the Sedgwick computations are put together they indicate that Elizabeth Freeman was born in 1744.

She was the first, or one of the first, of her race to achieve freedom from slavery by force of law in Massachusetts. She lived and died a heroine, in all of the bigger and better senses of the word.

HAROLD W. FELTON

I.
IN WHICH COLONEL ASHLEY HAS IMPORTANT VISITORS

BET'S WIDE APRON sparkled like new snow. A white cap glistened above her black face and hair like a rising cloud catching the full rays of a morning sun. Her neat gray dress was ironed smooth and the tips of her worn shoes, freshly shined, twinkled from under her hem as she walked.

She had prepared for this day with the greatest care, for visitors were in the house. Important visitors. Mr. Tapping Reeve had come from Litchfield, in Connecticut. Mr. Theodore Sedgwick was there too. He was a pleasant young man, a lawyer from Sheffield, a few miles away, on the Housatonic River. And there were several others.

Bet didn't know why they had all come to the Ashley House, but she knew it was an important meeting. Perhaps she would find out why the men had come when she served them.

Bet was a slave. She was owned by Colonel John Ashley. He had bought her when she was a baby, with her sister Lizzie and several other slaves. When she had married, her name became Freeman—Elizabeth Freeman—but everyone called her Bet.

Colonel Ashley's house was the only home she had ever known. She had lived a good life, perhaps as good as a slave can live. The Colonel was distant and stern, yet not unkind. Mistress Ashley ruled her kitchen and her house with a firm hand, a sharp tongue, a shrill voice, and a quick temper. Nevertheless, it was not a bad life, as slaves' lives went.

Everyone worked hard. The slaves took pride in their work. Lizzie and Bet had discovered they were happiest when they were busy, but poor Lizzie was sickly and not always able to keep up with her sister and the other slaves. It was Lizzie who most often felt the sharpness of Mistress Ashley's tongue. It was Lizzie who, because she was not strong and quick, brought Mistress Ashley's shrillest voice into the kitchen, and it was Lizzie who sometimes felt the heavy weight of Mistress Ashley's hand.

John Ashley was one of the first settlers in western Massachusetts. With a few others he had made the long, hard trip over the Berkshire Mountains, cutting a narrow road through the forests. He had organized the Town of Sheffield in the southwest corner of the Commonwealth.

In 1735 he had built the Ashley House, a mansion on the banks of the river, near Ashley Falls. He had married Hannah Hogeboom of Claverack, New York. A rich man, with a big house and a beautiful wife, John Ashley bought slaves from the Hogeboom family. Bet and her sister had been brought to Ashley House on the straw-covered bed of a sleigh when Bet was six months old.

John Ashley had built a grist mill on the Housatonic River. He had interests in iron mines and quarries. He owned a great deal of land in the fertile valley and in the heavily wooded hills where his men operated lumber mills and prepared charcoal for use in the furnaces where iron was made.

Colonel Ashley joined with Theodore Sedgwick and the other men in Sheffield and wrote a Declaration of Rights in 1773 which declared that "Mankind in a State of Nature are equal, free and independent of each other." A town meeting on February 25, 1774, was called to discuss "the present inhuman practise of enslaving our fellow creatures, the natives of Africa." Colonel Ashley also took a leading part in the Revolutionary War in western Massachusetts.

Bet had come to occupy an important place in the household. She was respected and trusted. Under Mistress Ashley's supervision, the kitchen and the house were in her charge. The herb garden grew green and fragrant under her care.

Whenever the political and social leaders met at Ashley House, as they often did, Bet heard them talk of freedom and equality. She knew that the war against England was being fought for those goals. She wondered when freedom would come and what she would do when it came.

She felt that she would stay with Colonel Ashley. She had a good home. She liked everything about it, except Mistress Ashley. But then, a person couldn't have everything. It was too bad that Mistress Ashley lost her temper and raised her voice so often. Bet would like to be able to look Mistress Ashley in the eye and tell her, "If you don't stop pickin' on Lizzie, I'm goin' to quit." Perhaps then Mistress Ashley would not mistreat poor Lizzie, because Bet was an excellent cook and housekeeper and Mistress Ashley would not like to lose her.

And so there came this day in the year 1780, a day when Bet, dressed in her best clothes, carried a heavy wooden tray loaded with bottles and pewter tankards and meat and bread and pickles into the huge study on the second floor of the Ashley House.

The men in the room were leaders in the community and in the Commonwealth. They were men who spoke for and fought for freedom and independence. The men of the Massachusetts Colony had always been in the lead in the fight for freedom.

Bet's husband had been in that same fight. He had fought and died as a soldier in the war for independence that was still going on. He had left her with a baby, Little Bet.

Bet knew about the Declaration of Independence that was adopted by the Continental Congress in Philadelphia on July 4, 1776. She had heard Colonel Ashley read the bold words it contained, and she had always felt her flesh tingle as he read. "We hold these Truths to be self-evident, that all Men are created equal, that they are endowed by their Creator with certain un-alienable Rights, that among these are Life, Liberty and the Pursuit of Happiness."

The pastor had preached about these things—equality, free-dom, and rights. Farmers at husking bees and house raisings spoke of them. So did their wives at quilting bees and harvest dinners.

Bet was sure it meant all women and children, as well as men. She didn't want Little Bet to grow up to be a slave. She wanted her baby to be free. Then she could learn to read and write and do sums. Then she could live and work in her own way and grow up to be a fine person, who could take part in community life.

The words held a promise to Bet during the days of war, when battles were fought north, south, east, and west of her home in Ashley Falls. They became filled with deeper meaning when the news came that her husband had died in the war. If he did not give his life for freedom, then he had given it for nothing at all.

Bet moved with quiet skill as she placed the shining tankards and bottles before the men, along with the platters of cold meat, bread, and the dishes of pickles. She felt excitement in the room.

"I am overjoyed that it is done," exclaimed Colonel Ashley. "Massachusetts has always led the way to independence and to freedom. This new constitution for Massachusetts is a noble document."

"True," said Mr. Tapping Reeve. "Massachusetts led the way at the Boston Tea Party. At Concord and at Lexington."

"And before that too," said Theodore Sedgwick. "The other Colonies have always followed Massachusetts. It is only fitting that Massachusetts have its new constitution contain a declaration of freedom and equality."

Bet placed a tankard before him. He looked up, smiled and said, "Thank you." Not every man paused to thank a slave and smile. Bet's face brightened and she responded to his pleasant greeting.

"You are right, Theodore," said Colonel Ashley. He picked up the paper from the table before him. "Ah. Here it is." He read slowly, impressively. "All men are born free and equal."

"Good," said Mr. Sedgwick. "The supreme law of Massachusetts."

As it always did when she heard such words, a tingle came at the nape of Bet's neck and a shiver ran down her spine. She lifted the tray, but had to set it down on the table to keep it from trembling out of control in her hands.

Over and over the words raced through her mind. "All men are created free and equal . . . the supreme law . . ."

Freedom was coming nearer. When would it finally come? Why didn't some of these men who were so happy with the idea of freedom talk to her about it? She was a slave. No one could understand freedom better than she. She hurriedly left the room to give thanks for those wonderful words and for the freedom that she felt was coming closer to her.

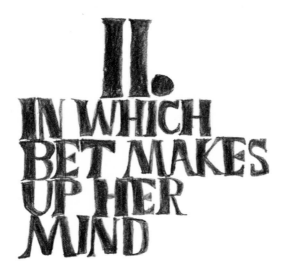

II.
IN WHICH BET MAKES UP HER MIND

THE MONTHS passed. Bet often wondered when someone would come and tell her she was free, that she was no longer a slave. If it was the law, someone ought to come and tell her about it.

She had discussed freedom with Lizzie and with Brom, the big Negro slave who cared for the yard and did the heavy work around the house. She talked about it with the other slaves too. Brom wanted his freedom almost as much as Bet did, but the others were not so sure. They wondered what they could do, how they could support themselves.

But there was not much time for wonder. There were meals to cook, laundry to be done, baking, ironing, scrubbing, polishing, sweeping, dusting, dishwashing, beds to be made, the herb garden to be tended. Yet if Bet's hands were always busy, so was her mind, and sometimes during the long, busy days, she did wonder.

Bet had spent an active day and now dinner was cooking in the great open fireplace in the kitchen. Lizzie had been sick all the night before and had felt weak since morning. Bet had not stopped all day, trying to do Lizzie's work, as well as her own.

From the pantry she heard Mistress Ashley screaming at Lizzie. Bet couldn't understand the words, so great was the anger in the voice, but the harsh sound went on and on, louder, more bitter, more uncontrolled. If only there was some way to stop that ill-humored voice. But what could Bet do?

She wanted to leave, to run away where she couldn't hear. But she couldn't do that. She couldn't leave Lizzie there alone with a woman in a tantrum.

Bet opened the pantry door. A terrible sight met her eyes. Lizzie was crouched near the kitchen table, on the floor. Mistress Ashley stood by the fireplace. She held the heavy iron shovel above her head. It glowed red with heat. Hot ashes were falling to the polished floor.

Bet rushed forward, and put out her arm to ward off the blow. The shovel fell and its hard metal edge struck her arm, cutting it to the bone. A red stain spread down her torn sleeve. Blood splashed to the kitchen floor like crimson drops of rain. A sharp cry of pain towered above the bitter words and the clatter of metal as the shovel fell on the hearthstone.

Colonel Ashley hurried down from his study. Brom came on the run to find out what had happened.

Bet was filled with a great calm. Her mind was made up. She had decided what she was going to do as quickly as she had stepped in front of the falling shovel. She would find out about this new constitution. It said all men were born free and equal. But here she was, a slave. She was not free and she was not equal. Something was wrong, very wrong.

Bet had heard the lawyers and the other gentlemen talk. They all agreed it was right that the new Massachusetts constitution declared everyone was born free and equal. If no one else enforced the law, if no one else made the new constitution mean what it said, Bet would do it. She didn't know how. But she would do it. She would find a way.

She told Lizzie and Brom what she intended to do. Brom asked that she speak for him too, but Lizzie was afraid. She didn't know what she could do unless she had the home Colonel Ashley gave her.

On a cold, wet day, Bet trudged through the heavy black mud. She carried Little Bet in her arms. It was four miles to the village of Sheffield. Mr. Sedgwick was a lawyer. He was the only lawyer she knew who might help her. Perhaps he could do something.

A refrain filled her mind as she moved her tired feet, weighted with mud. The words came to her again and again as the rain

lashed at her. All men are born free and equal—free and equal
—free and equal—

Theodore Sedgwick was seated in the small room that was
his law office. He was still a young man and not many clients
had made their way to his door.

"Come in," he said when he heard a firm, measured knock.

When the door opened and he saw Bet standing in the en-
trance, her clothes soaked with the cold spring rain, the book
he was holding in his hands fell to the table with a thump.

"Why, Bet! Goodness! Come in, come in. Take your wet
cloak off. Have a chair." He went to her. She put the baby on
a bench and removed her dripping cloak.

His greeting warmed her almost as much as the fire, for she
had not known how she would be received. She still did not
know, for that matter, as she had not yet told him the purpose
of her visit. She wondered how to tell him, how to start. She
didn't have to wonder long. He asked the question.

"It is good to see you, Bet. How does it happen you are so
far from the Ashley House? With Little Bet too? I hope nothing
is wrong there?"

Bet straightened in her chair. "I am so far from the Ashley
House, Mr. Sedgwick, because I want to be free," she said.

It was a simple statement and the words were clear, but she
had said something that took them both into a strange and un-
known world. Negro slaves were not made free because they
wanted freedom. The law had recognized slavery in the American Colonies ever since they were founded. Slavery was an in-

stitution, a part of a way of life.

Theodore Sedgwick perhaps had never thought of a slave trying to become free. "Well now, I don't know," was all he was able to say.

But if his mind was slow to grasp the point, Bet was quick to explain. "The Massachusetts constitution says that everybody is born free and equal," she declared.

"Yes, but—you are a slave and slaves are—" His words were slow in forming. He had been happy with the new constitution, but he had not thought of how a black slave might have freedom.

"I'm a person. I'm not a dumb beast. I was born, but I'm not free. The constitution ought to mean what it says, and I want you to go to law for me and get the law to say I'm free."

"Whatever gave you this idea, Bet?"

"I got it by keepin' still and mindin' things. I've heard you and other gentlemen talk at Colonel Ashley's house, and I've thought about it a lot," Bet answered.

"But it can't be simple, it can't—"

"I don't know 'can't.' The constitution says all men are free and equal, doesn't it?"

"Well, yes—"

"Then if everybody is free, there can't be any slaves, because slaves aren't free. Then when Mistress Ashley did what she did—"

The young lawyer listened as Bet told him what had happened in the Ashley House that day.

There had always been slavery in Massachusetts—indeed, in

every colony in North America. Theodore Sedgwick had been active in the cause of freedom for slaves. He had wondered what effect the new constitution of Massachusetts would have on slavery. He was a sensitive, thoughtful man, but many such men found little objection to slavery as it was practiced in western Massachusetts and in most of the country areas of the northern states. There, black slaves and free white working people lived on the same level, wore the same kind of clothes, lived in the same kind of houses. Indeed, a slave of a wealthy master such as Colonel Ashley lived better than many white people.

But perhaps he had never realized the depth of the love of freedom in black people, even those as fortunate as Bet. He knew that blacks were fighting in General Washington's army, and everywhere were working with their masters to win the war. Possibly it had never occurred to him that their hearts led them to fight so well and do so much because they too dreamed of their own freedom as a goal.

It may be that he had not deeply considered that the black people of America, like the white people, also were suffering through a long, hard war and also sought their own rights of life, liberty, and the pursuit of happiness.

As he looked at Bet, the fact that she had lost her soldier husband in the war took on a new, a fuller meaning.

How was it to be done? What legal proceedings? What arguments?

If he had never thought of these things before, he did now.

His mind was caught by Bet's simple intensity and the logic of her words.

"I've talked to Brom. He wants to be free too," Bet added. "Can't you do something for us?"

There was a sound on the doorstep. The door opened and a gush of cold, wet wind broke into the room. It was John Ashley and his son. "Come with us, Bet," said Colonel Ashley. His voice was firm.

Bet rose and turned toward him. "I am free and equal," she said evenly.

"You are a slave," he said.

"The constitution says I'm free and equal," she replied, and her voice rose, burning with intensity.

"You are my servant for life," said John Ashley.

Bet turned to Theodore Sedgwick. Her face was alive with question.

"I'm afraid you will have to go with them," said Theodore Sedgwick.

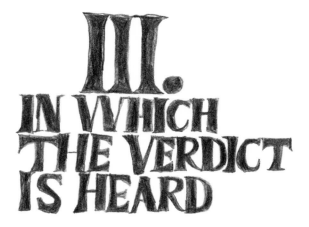

II.
IN WHICH THE VERDICT IS HEARD

JOHN ASHLEY was not a cruel man. He owned slaves because he was rich and could afford to buy them. With their work, he became richer, and their toil made life easier for him and his family. His slaves lived well. They lived in comfort, compared to many other working people.

Of course Mistress Ashley should not have struck Bet. But then many families, most families, have trouble now and then and quarrels, even violent quarrels, were not uncommon.

Slaves were property. That had always been true in America and a man was entitled to his property. Ashley did not believe that the law should take property from him. He had cared for his slaves when they were children. He would care for them when they were too old to work. Black people could not support themselves alone, he thought. As farm laborers, there would be no work for them in the winter, and only a few people could afford to hire a woman for housework.

He felt sympathy for Bet and tried to cheer her up. In the days that followed he did his best to explain that his wife was sorry she had lost her temper. Indeed, Hannah Ashley tearfully apologized.

Bet was forlorn. She wanted to forgive Mistress Ashley and she did forgive the poor woman who had so little control of herself. Yet Bet wanted her freedom. She didn't know what she would do as a free person. She would find it difficult, maybe impossible, to find work for wages. She would be lucky to find a place to live as comfortable as the Ashley household.

The long days passed. She was closely watched and had no way of again talking with Mr. Sedgwick, or anyone else who might help her. She began to think it was foolish to believe that anyone would come to her aid. Who would help a slave with no money and no property? Her heart was filled with emptiness as she went about her daily chores.

Still, Bet knew, little that is good or hoped for comes easily. The war had started in 1775. It was now spring of 1781, and still it went on. And before the years of the war there had been years of negotiation and the heartbreak that comes with failure. Yet the Colonists continued to fight.

Bet did not know how much her visit had turned Mr. Sedgwick's mind to thought and question. He spent long hours pouring over law books. He discussed the problem with Mr. Tapping Reeve.

One busy morning Bet answered a knock at the door. A man she recognized as the sheriff of the county stood on the stoop. "You are Bet?" he asked.

"Yes sir," she replied.

"Is a man here by the name of Brom?"

"Yes sir. He's in the barn or in the garden, probably."

"I have a writ of replevin for both of you from the Inferior Court of Common Pleas," he said as he drew a paper from his pocket.

Replevin. Common Pleas. Inferior Court. Most of these were words she had never heard. But—court. She knew that word. A flood of excitement trembled through her body.

"Is Colonel Ashley in?" the sheriff asked.

"Yes sir. I'll call him. Won't you step in?" Bet led the man to the sitting room and went upstairs to tell the Colonel of the visitor.

Colonel Ashley hurried down the stairs. Bet followed him.

"Good day, Colonel. I have a writ of replevin for Bet and Brom," the sheriff said.

"They are my servants for life," Colonel Ashley said.

"I must take them with me." The sheriff handed the paper to the Colonel.

The Colonel glanced at the paper. "I will not permit it," he said curtly.

"I am ordered by the court to take them," the man said firmly. Bet wondered how he dared to continue after the Colonel had spoken so sharply. Colonel Ashley was a lawyer, and although he did not practice law, his library was filled with important looking law books. How could anyone ever hope to overcome Colonel Ashley?

Her master replied again. "I will not permit them to leave with you. They are my chattels, my property."

There was a pause that almost suffocated Bet. Colonel Ashley turned to her. "Tell the sheriff you will not go with him, Bet," he said.

Bet felt she would sink through the floor. She had never disobeyed a direct order of her master. However, she drew herself up straight. Courteously and firmly she forced herself to say, "Colonel Ashley, sir, I want my freedom, like the constitution says."

She was surprised at herself, surprised she could speak out, speak her mind to the Colonel.

Colonel Ashley was just as direct, just as firm. "I will not permit you to leave," he said.

"I will have to report this to the court," the sheriff said.

"Do that. Say to the court that if they are to go, I must have security. I must have a bond. They are my property. I do not have to surrender my property without a proper bond."

The sheriff moved to the door. Bet opened it for him. He turned to Colonel Ashley. "Thank you, Colonel," he said. "Good day."

Colonel Ashley nodded. Bet was left alone with him. She was not sure what had happened. She did not know about courts and sheriffs, but she felt that Mr. Sedgwick must not have forgotten her after all. In the silence, despair came over her.

"I don't want you to leave the house, Bet," Colonel Ashley said. "Do you understand?"

What could be done now? Colonel Ashley owned a thousand acres of land, the grist mill, saw mills, so many other things. He had dozens of servants and tenants and there were scores of other men he could call upon. Certainly, no one could rescue her. Mr. Sedgwick had sought the help of the law and the law had failed. It could never succeed against a man as powerful as Colonel Ashley. The small glow of hope that had flickered within her was gone.

But Bet did not know the ways of the law. In a few days the sheriff once more rode into the backyard. Several men were with him.

"May I see Colonel Ashley?" he said as he stood at the door.

"Yes sir," Bet replied, and went for the Colonel.

When the Colonel appeared on the stoop, he greeted the officer who handed him some papers. One bore a red seal of wax and two small red ribbons fluttered from it. It was a writ of replevin, an order of the Inferior Court of Common Pleas at Great Barrington. There was also a bond for security.

The Colonel spoke to Bet. "The court has ordered me to let you and Brom go with the sheriff. I ask you to remain with us."

Bet said simply, "Colonel Ashley, I want to be free."

Brom had drawn close. He had heard the conversation. "Me too," he said. "I want to be free too."

"Yes, Brom. The writ includes you too," his master said.

"I'll come back and work for you when I am free," Brom said.

"You'll be glad to have steady employment if you do get your freedom. But I doubt that you will," said Colonel Ashley.

He turned to Bet. "Haven't we given you a good home?" he asked.

"Yes," Bet replied.

"Good food?"

"Yes sir,"

"Good clothing?"

"Yes sir."

Mistress Ashley had come out on the porch. "I am sorry, Bet. I apologize humbly for what I did," she said. "We want you to be happy."

"I forgive you, Mistress Ashley. I do. But I want my freedom."

"Where will you find another home as good?"

"I don't know," said Bet. "Maybe I won't find one. Maybe I'll live in rags and starve. But I want to be free and equal, like the constitution says."

The sheriff took Bet, with Little Bet, and Brom to the court where Mr. Sedgwick soon appeared. The legal details were cared for. It was May. The trial would be in August. Brom got a job with a farmer until the trial. But Bet was in a different position. She was a woman with a baby.

Colonel Ashley was right. There seemed to be no place for Bet to stay, nothing for her to do, no job.

"Come home with me," said Mr. Sedgwick. "You may stay with us until we can find something for you to do. It is now late May. Your case will not come up before court until August."

Three small children were in the house. Eliza was six, Frances was three, and little Theodore was almost six months old. Mr. Sedgwick's wife was a frail woman. The servants were careless and worked without instruction. The household was untidy.

It seemed that magic entered Theodore Sedgwick's home. It was the magic of Bet's enthusiasm, her skill in management, her wholesome approach to life and the people about her.

Now the children were always clean and happy. Meals were served on time. Furniture took on a new shine, pewter bore a deeper, richer glow, silver sparkled. Floors glistened, hearthstones were swept, the linen was spotless. Beds were made and changed at the proper time. The whole household gleamed. Stain, strain, argument, and unhappiness sped away. Bet's influence was everywhere. She was a happy and contented person once more, and cared for Eliza, Frances, and Theodore as though they were her own.

Mr. Sedgwick was deep in political and business matters. He was often away from home. When he returned he always found that his household and family had received devoted and loving care in his absence.

On an August day in 1781, Bet and Brom, with Theodore Sedgwick and Tapping Reeve from Litchfield, went to the court in Great Barrington. There, before the judge, they met Colonel John Ashley and his lawyers.

Bet seemed calm as the lawyers went about their affairs in the conduct of the trial, but a great turmoil was within her as the jury was selected and Jonathan Holcomb was named foreman.

Bet had lived on the western frontier all her life. She knew people often disagreed with each other. Sometimes disagreement led to fights and warfare. The Indian wars and the Revolutionary War were fought because people could not agree. As the August sun, shining through the windows, spread neat patterns of light on the floor of the courtroom, she was moved with the simplicity and the beauty of this peaceful way of settling disputes. She wondered why all men at all times could not find the answer to their problems in law instead of conflict.

"I am troubled, Bet," Mr. Sedgwick whispered.

"About my trial?" Bet asked.

"Yes."

"There's no reason for that." Bet replied.

Mr. Sedgwick looked at her curiously. "Why do you say that?" he asked.

If Mr. Sedgwick was troubled about legal points, Bet was not. "The constitution says all people are free and equal. If that is so, how can I, how can anybody, be a slave?" she said.

Mr. Sedgwick smiled and nodded. Here was a remarkable

woman. She would have made a good lawyer, he thought.

"There is no law that makes me a slave. You told me that."

"That's right. But there are laws about slaves. And there is custom, and custom is sometimes stronger than law," he said.

"There's nothin' about custom in the constitution. Jes' you tell those things to the judge and jury in lawyer words. Then everything will be all right."

She heard the evidence and the arguments of the lawyers and no outward sign betrayed the tension that filled her. Her future was at stake. She lived in Massachusetts and she was testing the law of the land she lived in. As the trial went on a great feeling of serenity replaced all the disturbing emotions of the past months.

The judge listened. The jury leaned forward in their seats so that no word would escape them.

Bet sighed with soft contentment when she heard the verdict. She was not the servant of John Ashley for her lifetime. She was awarded thirty shillings lawful silver money as damages, and for costs, five pounds, fourteen shillings, and four pence.

Soon she was alone with Mr. Sedgwick in the silent courtroom. "You have been given damages for your services since you were twenty-one years old, and costs. What shall I do with the money?" Mr. Sedgwick asked with a smile.

"Pay Mr. Reeve and pay yourself for your lawyers' fees. Pay well because now I have the dearest thing on earth—my freedom. Then, I'd be obliged to you if you will keep what may be left for me. Keep it so I can use it if I need it."

No one was waiting to cheer her for her great victory. There was only Brom to grasp her hand in friendship. But Massachusetts and the County of Berkshire had done their part. They had fulfilled the promise of the constitution. Bet was a free person!

There was no doubt what she would do now. She was so much needed, so completely capable. She, with Little Bet, remained in the Sedgwick household. To the satisfaction of everyone, she became the gentle, intelligent force behind its daily operation.

Lizzie did not want to leave Ashley House. When Bet had asked her about it, she said, "Oh, no. I wouldn't want to leave. Mistress Ashley has been nice to me lately. She doesn't scold so much any more. I'd be afraid to leave Colonel Ashley's house."

The months became years and the Sedgwick family moved to Stockbridge. Theodore Sedgwick's law practice grew rapidly after his success in handling Bet's case. More and more clients sought his services as a lawyer. The size of the family increased.

To the children who depended on the black woman so much, the one who cared for them so tenderly, she became Mumbet, or Mama Bet. Soon she was Mumbet not only to the children, but to the parents, friends, and neighbors. It was a name that fixed Bet's position in the family, a name created of honor, of respect, of love.

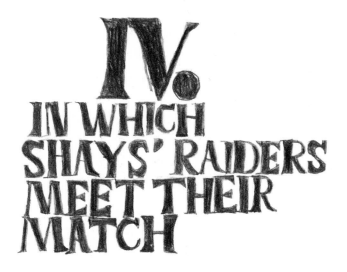

IV.
IN WHICH SHAYS' RAIDERS MEET THEIR MATCH

HARD TIMES came. Many workmen were without jobs. Money was scarce. Farmers found it difficult to pay their debts and taxes. It was 1786. The United States had won the war and was independent of England. But the states were loosely organized. The Federal Government had only limited powers under Articles of Confederation. The Congress was struggling to create a stable government. The Federal Constitution would not be ratified until 1789.

Rebellion against the Government smoldered in the hearts of men who, a half dozen years before, had won a war of rebellion against a king.

Daniel Shays led the rebellion in Massachusetts. Unfortunately, as is often the case, mob action took the place of protest and discussion. Unruly men took to the roads intent on plunder. Mortgages had been foreclosed. Property had been sold to collect debts. The rebels made for the courts and for the homes of the wealthy. Columns of black smoke pushing into the sky, like dark exclamation points, punctuated the horizon and told of fires that sometimes came with the rebels.

Judge Theodore Sedgwick had been elected to the Congress and was away from home on Government business. He had been in active opposition to Shays' followers and the rebels had often threatened his life.

Mumbet was in the house alone with Mrs. Sedgwick and the children. Mrs. Sedgwick was ill, in bed.

Mumbet saw a column of smoke far up the road. She saw people hurry past the house. The news spread. A gang of Shays' men was coming.

She called the children and they came running. "Come on, now. I want you to go to your mother's room. You go along too, Little Bet. Shays' men are comin'." She followed them as they trooped up the stairs.

"What is it, Bet?" Mrs. Sedgwick asked as they filed into her room.

"Shays' rebels are comin'. I think the children should stay with you."

"Oh, dear," Mrs. Sedgwick moaned helplessly. "What will we do?"

"Jes' leave it to me. I'll try to take care of 'em. I hope I can keep their minds away from settin' fire to anything, or breakin' or stealin' anything."

Mrs. Sedgwick's eyes opened wide with fear and burned dark against her pale face. Her hands fluttered helplessly above the sheets.

"Don't you worry." Mumbet's calmness and her proven ability to take care of things quieted the ill woman.

"Now you children, you jes' stay right here. Don't leave the room, and don't you be scared."

After she closed the door she moved quickly through the house. She hid the wine and the spirits in a dark corner in the cellar but left the porter stacked in neat rows on a shelf in the pantry. Smiling grimly, she selected the bottles of porter that had gone flat and put them in the front row. Flat porter was very bitter and she hoped its bitterness might discourage drinking, if the men found it.

Returning upstairs, she gathered up the silver, stuffing it into pillow cases. Then she carried the heavy load to her room on the top floor. There, she put it all in a large pine chest that stood by the wall near her sewing table. She covered the silver with blankets and quilts she had made and piled her winter clothes on top.

Satisfied that she had done the best she could, she locked the pine chest and stuffed the key beneath the handkerchief in the bottom of one of her apron's big pockets. She gave it a firm pat as though the treasure were safely stowed away in a bank vault.

Then Mumbet moved to the window and peered out. She had finished her work just in time. A group of men on horseback were coming down the road toward the house.

As she went rapidly down the stairs she heard loud voices in the yard. "I've got to be as nice to 'em as I can," she muttered softly to herself. "But—" She picked up the long, heavy kitchen fireplace shovel she had brought from the back of the house and gripped it firmly.

The voices were louder now. She heard the tramp of hard-soled shoes coming across the porch. Mumbet stood silently in the hall, waiting.

The front door trembled under heavy blows. Mumbet stiffened. Her porch floor was being scuffed, her door was being marked—the floor and the door she had polished and cleaned so carefully.

She strode to the door, opened it wide, and stood squarely in the frame, the long shovel held solidly in her hand. A dozen rough men stood before her. "What do you mean by knockin' your gun butt against my door?" she demanded. "No use in that! There's a knocker. Next time, use it!"

The mob standing before her had not expected so firm a response. None of them seemed to have a voice. "What do you want?" she asked sternly.

The leader, a tall man with a dark beard, found words. "Where's Judge Sedgwick?" he asked in a rough voice.

"He's not here," Bet said with a scowl.

"He's here all right," one of the men insisted.

"Yeah. An' we want him," another said.

Bet's shovel moved slightly, but dangerously. "I said he's not here, an' I mean what I say," she said firmly.

"Search the house," came a voice from the crowd. "Search it for arms and ammunition too!"

"Yeah. Search it. If we can't find no guns or the judge, there's always the silver."

"Let's search it."

"Yeah. Get goin'."

"Push her out of the way."

"Don't you dare touch me!" Mumbet said defiantly. "Don't you dare strike a woman, not even a poor old black woman!"

There was a long silence. Then feet scuffled against the floor as the crowd pushed toward her.

"We came here to find the judge," a voice insisted from the rear of the crowd.

"We got to search, ma'am," the leader said.

Ma'am! That was a good sign. At least they had not knocked her aside. Her firmness had prevented that. And at least one of them had some small courtesy in him. She would not retreat. She would show no fright. She would control them. At least, if a show of courage and firmness would control them, she would do it.

"Well," she said as she looked calmly at the hard faces. "I tell you Judge Sedgwick is not here. He's off, tryin' to make a better government for us, while you're here tryin' to tear it down. Nobody's here except me and the children and Mrs.

Sedgwick, and she's sick. I'll show you around and you can search all you want to. But don't you go and do any damage and don't you get Mrs. Sedgwick upset or she'll get real sick, real bad again." The quick sentences were firm commands. The shovel danced slightly, but menacingly.

Mumbet stood aside as the men moved into the wide hall. She noticed that some of them took off their hats and stuffed them in their pockets. Humph! Some of them have at least got a little bit of gentleman in them, she thought. But they were hard, rough men and they had only started their search. She still had a far distance to go with them.

"Where's the guns an' ammunition?" the leader asked.

"There's none that I know of here," said Mumbet. "The Judge took all that stuff to his office, or somewhere."

"Where's the silver?" he demanded as he saw the bare shelves and sideboard.

"Put away somewhere," Mumbet answered. She was glad he didn't ask her where it had been put. Why was it that these people felt they had to fight and destroy and steal things? There were better ways to right wrongs and correct injustices. She had proven that by going to court to get her freedom. But her thoughts were quickly interrupted.

"Look in the drawers for the silver. Look in all the closets. Look under everything." The leader's commands were brisk.

"I jest want to get my hands on that silver," one of the men said as he pushed his hands into a big drawer.

"Sure. The Judge is loaded with it," another said.

The men went quickly through the first floor. In the cellar one of them paused in the pantry. "Hey, look at this!" He reached for a bottle among the many stacked on the shelf before him.

"Bottles! Let me have one!"

"Me too!"

The man who held the bottle struck its neck against a stone in the wall of the pantry.

Bet heard the voice and the crash of glass. This was a dangerous moment. If they found the spirits, such men would be very difficult. She must act. "Wait a minute!" she cried as she shouldered her way through the crowd. Her shovel pointed the way. She glared at the man holding the broken bottle.

"That's porter. If you want some, I'll fetch a corkscrew and draw the cork. I'll give you some—in a glass. Then you can drink it like you were a gentleman!"

She took the broken bottle from the speechless man. Then, picking up one of the bottles with flat porter, she moved toward the glasses.

Carefully Mumbet put a few glasses on a tray, opened the bottle of flat porter, poured some of it into a glass and offered it to the rowdy who had broken the bottle. "We always entertain everybody who comes to this house, and we offer them what we have—whether they know how to act like gentlemen or not. If you are thirsty, you are more than welcome to a drink."

The man took the glass and tasted the liquid. "Phew! That's

bitter stuff!" he exclaimed. "If gentlemen drink such cursed sour stuff, they can keep it. If that's what gentlemen drink, I'm glad I ain't one."

"You've got no problems about that," Mumbet sniffed. "Is anyone else thirsty?" Her dark, flashing eyes moved over the crowd.

A few of the men tasted the flat porter, but it was a drink they were not familiar with and they found it much too bitter for their taste.

"Now, you are welcome to search the cellar—but don't you damage anything, or I'll skin you alive!" The shovel moved menacingly.

After all the men came up from the cellar, she stopped them in the kitchen. "Like I told you, only Mrs. Sedgwick and the children are upstairs."

"The Judge is in the closet in her room, eh?" the leader said.

"Along with the silver," another added.

"No he's not and it's not. But if you think you jes' have to take a look, two of you can do it. There's no reason for all of you to go traipsin' around in her room and disturbin' a poor sick woman."

"All right," the leader said. "Let's go upstairs. Only two of us will search her room."

"This way then. Be quiet—and don't scuff my floors! Pick up your feet when you walk!" She glared at them and the rough men followed her meekly as she led the way.

She stopped in front of Mrs. Sedgwick's door as the other

rooms were searched. When they returned to the hall, Mumbet said, "Excuse me. I'll be right back." She opened the door and entered the room.

"They want to search the room, but only two of them will come in," she said.

"Oh my! Oh dear!" Mrs. Sedgwick said, pulling the bed clothes up closely around her.

"They won't cause trouble. Not so long as I've got breath in my body," Bet said quietly and with a firmness that did not permit of doubt. "Children, you stand close to your mother. You too, Little Bet. Don't be afraid." She shepherded them to the bed.

"Come in," she said, opening the door.

Two men entered, embarrassed, trying not to see Mrs. Sedgwick and the children. After a quick look in the closets and the bureau drawers, they turned toward the door. "Aren't you goin' to look under the bed?" Mumbet asked, her voice dripping with sarcasm.

They paused, looking at each other, and finally stooped down to peer under the bed. Then they went out, Mumbet following them.

"Now where's the silver?" the leader demanded, turning to face the black woman.

"The Judge knew Shays' men were on the loose in the country before he went away. No doubt he hid it or had someone hide it," she replied.

"What's on the top floor?" the leader asked, looking up the stairway.

"My room and the children's playroom," Mumbet answered.

"Come on. Let's take a look."

Mumbet led them up the stairs and quickly the closets and the drawers in the children's playroom were searched. When she went into her own room, she sank down on the pine chest with a heavy sigh, and as she sat, she began to wipe her face with her handkerchief and fan herself with it.

Her closet suffered the indignity of search. "What's in the chest?" the leader asked.

"This is my chest," Mumbet said.

"We'll jest take a look."

"Sure. Take a look. You been takin' plenty of looks, scuffin' my floors an' makin' a nuisance of yourselves. Now you want to look in a poor old black lady's pine chest." Her voice was sharp.

"Why—"

Mumbet didn't know what the man was going to say, but she didn't give him a chance to finish or to think.

"What kind of men are you anyway? Pretty small, I can see that. Why you haven't even looked under my bed yet. It's right there. Why don't you look underneath it? The silver might be there. Or even the Judge might be there," she scoffed.

"Here I've been escortin' you all through this house, showin' you everything you want to see, lettin' you search your way from the cellar to the attic to your hearts' content, with you

messin' up my floors and things that I work so hard to keep smooth and shinin' an' clean." She breathed a huge sigh that seemed a part of her long speech.

She didn't stop talking. "Now you've got me all tuckered out. And here I am, a poor old black woman, poorer than any of you, if the truth was known, probably. All worn out from watchin' you do all your foolishness." She sighed at the distress of it all, but the high note of scorn never left her voice.

"I told you in the beginning you wouldn't find the Judge and that you wouldn't find any silver. But no. You wouldn't believe me. And now, the first time I get a chance to catch my breath you want to go pokin' around in a poor old lady's pine chest. I declare, I never— What big, brave men you are! Real heroes, I bet. Why don't you look under my bed first?" she repeated. "Very likely you'll find the Judge. Then you can go pokin' around in my pine chest among my winter petticoats!"

She did not pause often, but when she did, the very silence in the pauses carried contempt that cut deep. But no matter how much she talked, Mumbet did not move from her place on the pine chest. It seemed clear that she would talk all the rest of the day and all night if the men who faced her would only stand and listen.

"Come on, let's go," someone of the crowd said.

"Sure. Come on."

The leader paused. Mumbet held her breath, but she had stored up within her another torrent of reason, of words, of argument, and still more scorn.

"All right," the man said. "Come on. Why do we want to go pokin' around through her things?"

Mumbet remained firmly on her pine chest until the last of the men trailed out of the room. Then she followed them downstairs, her fire shovel still waving like a rattlesnake ready to strike.

In the lower hall, she passed ahead and courteously held the door open. Her face was stern, and she had not dropped the firm pose that had held them under control. She smiled inwardly when some of the men touched their foreheads and muttered, "Thank you, ma'am" as they filed out before her.

V.

IN WHICH MUMBET'S PLACE IN HISTORY IS ASSURED

THE ORDEAL was not over. One of the men, as he rounded the corner of the house, shouted, "Look at that horse!"

He was looking at Jenny Gray, Judge Sedgwick's best riding mare standing near the corner of the barn lot.

"That horse is mine! I'm goin' to take her!" he cried.

Mumbet's heart stopped for an awful moment. They were going to steal Jenny Gray. The Judge's heart would be broken and so would hers, for Jenny Gray was one of her pets and her favorite riding horse too. With Judge Sedgwick away in Boston or Philadelphia so much, Mumbet had full use of the mare.

The men scrambled off the porch and rushed toward the

barn lot. The man who had said he was going to take Jenny Gray was in the lead. Mumbet knew that the mare could not escape capture as long as she was penned up in the small lot. She hurried after the men.

When she reached the barn gate, the big, rawboned man with a dirty, grizzled growth of red beard, had seized a rope and was chasing after Jenny Gray. Mumbet shuddered at the thought of the beautiful mare being under the control of such a ruffian.

She ran out into the lot. "Here, here. That's no way to catch her," she cried. The red-bearded man stopped.

"That mare has got spirit. If you chase her like that you'll scare her so much she'll try to jump the fence and hurt herself. Give me that rope. Get out of here and I'll catch her."

The man dropped the rope and walked back to the gate. Jenny Gray, her head high, ears alert, and eyes flashing, stood in the distant corner of the lot. "Now you all go over and stand at the side of the barn where she can't see you. Jes' give her a minute to quiet down an' I'll catch her." Mumbet snapped out the instructions.

The tone of her voice and her complete assurance did not leave room for argument. The men trooped to the side of the barn like a group of schoolboys caught swiping apples.

After a pause, Mumbet whistled softly. "Here, Jenny. Come, Jenny," she called gently.

The beautiful gray mare lifted her head, and with a snort and a shake of her mane, trotted toward the black woman. As she approached, Mumbet held out her hand. The mare nuzzled

against her arm and she slipped the rope around her neck, holding it by the two ends. The gray horse walked willingly with
Mumbet toward the barn.

When she turned the corner the men were waiting. The gate
to the highway was open directly ahead.

As she walked, the horse at her side, Mumbet reached up as
though to fix her hair with one hand, and removed a hairpin.
"Here's your horse," she said. The men moved toward her, the
bearded one in the lead.

"Careful! You'll scare her," Mumbet cried, and at the same
time, she jabbed the sharp point of her hairpin into the mare's
side. She was standing between the men and the horse and they
could not see the hand that held the pin. The animal jumped.
As she did so Mumbet let one end of the rope slip.

"She's goin' to get away!"

"Hold her!"

"Hang on!"

But all the advice came too late. The mare was off and out
in the road and gone in half a dozen great leaps and a hammer
of hoof beats against the hard ground. She was free and fright-
ened. The memory of the sharp point of Mumbet's hairpin
would stay with her for a long time.

"What did you scare her for?" Mumbet demanded as she
adjusted her hair and slipped the pin back into place. No one
had noticed what she had done.

"I caught her for you and then you went and scared her
away!" She stood with her hands on her hips, watching Jenny

Gray run down the road, nostrils flaring, mane waving like a flag of victory behind her high-held head.

"Honest, I never saw such men! Didn't I tell you she's a high-spirited animal? You can't rush up at a high-bred horse that way!"

"Call her again," the man with the red beard said, angry that his prize had escaped.

"Won't do any good," Mumbet said. "You scared her too much. Goodness! I don't think anyone can ever catch her now that she's out in the road, what with all the open fields and all."

"Come on. We've got to go," the leader said. "Too bad you lost your mare, Red."

Mumbet knew the nags they rode could never catch up with Jenny Gray even if they tried to catch her. She knew also that the handsome gray horse would come back home soon after the wild strangers had left.

The ruffians moved northward. Mumbet looked south toward the way Jenny Gray had taken. "Sorry I had to give you such a jab, Jenny," she said softly. "But it was the only way I could keep those fellows from stealing you. I'll make it up to you and give you some maple sugar before you have your oats tonight."

Jenny Gray, although half a mile away, must have understood because already she had turned and was coming back toward her friend who stood alone at the side of the road, waiting for her.

Mumbet's influence spread through the Sedgwick family to

the next generation. In her later years, working as a nurse, she supported and educated her grandchildren and great-grand-children. In her own house, she continued to be considered a member of the Sedgwick family. Her character, her skill, her energy and her wonderful human qualities brought her the affection of the people of her community, the rich and the poor, the ordinary people and the famous.

When she died she was buried in the family circle in the Sedgwick cemetery lot in Stockbridge. Charles, the youngest Sedgwick son, was the author of the legend on the stone that stands at her grave:

ELIZABETH FREEMAN
known by the name of
MUMBET
died Dec. 28, 1829
Her supposed age
was 85 Years.
She was born a slave and remained
a slave for nearly thirty years. She
could neither read nor write yet in
her own sphere she had no superior
nor equal. She neither wasted time
nor property. She never violated a
trust nor failed to perform a duty.
In every situation of domestic trial,
she was the most efficient helper and
the tenderest friend. Good mother
farewell.

THE AUTHOR

HAROLD W. FELTON, a lawyer by profession, has long been interested in American folklore, and the first of his widely acclaimed books was an anthology of legends about Paul Bunyan. Since that time he has pursued folk heroes and tall tales with enthusiasm, and his stories for young people about Pecos Bill, John Henry, Fire-Fightin' Mose, Bowleg Bill, and Sergeant O'Keefe rank him as a master yarn-spinner.

In A HORSE NAMED JUSTIN MORGAN and WILLIAM PHIPS AND THE TREASURE SHIP, Mr. Felton dealt with facts that seemed like tall tales—history that was "almost too good to be true." In researching the stories of Jim Beckwourth, Edward Rose, and Nat Love, he discovered the same sort of material—biographies more astonishing than fiction.

Born in the Midwest, this popular author lives in New York City where he devotes his leisure time to writing.

THE ILLUSTRATOR

DONN ALBRIGHT was born in Muncie, Indiana, and attended art school on the West Coast. He is now a free-lance artist in New York City, and teaches illustration at Pratt Institute. His work has appeared in national magazines as well as in trade books and textbooks. Aside from his art work, his interests include science fiction, old comics, today's politics, and cats.